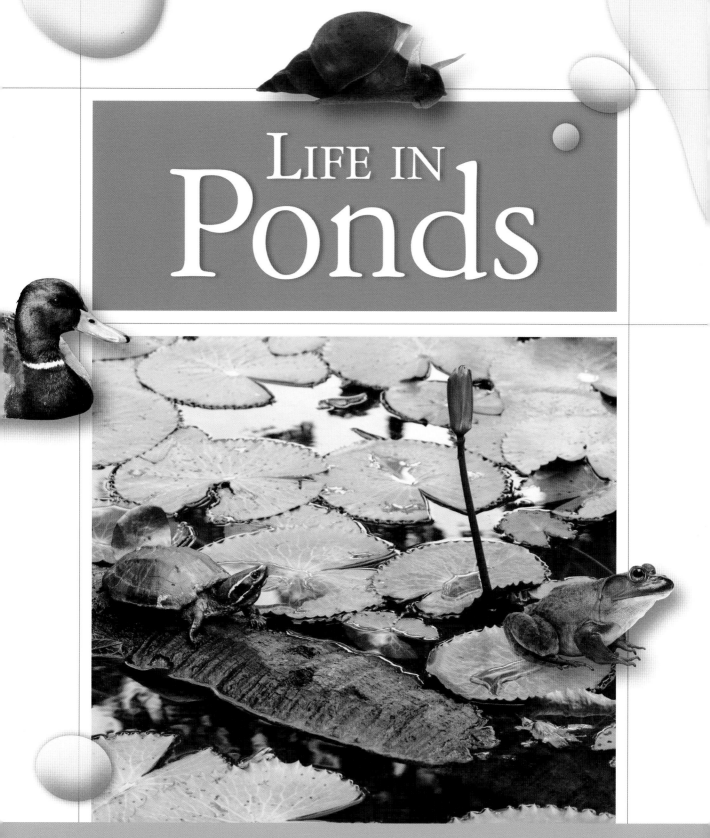

LIFE IN
Ponds

BY LAUREN COSS

Published by The Child's World®
1980 Lookout Drive • Mankato, MN 56003-1705
800-599-READ • www.childsworld.com

Acknowledgments
The Child's World®: Mary Berendes, Publishing Director
Red Line Editorial: Editorial direction
The Design Lab: Design
Amnet: Production

Design Elements: Shutterstock Images; Eric Isselee/Shutterstock
Images; Michiel de Wit/Shutterstock Images

Photographs ©: Shutterstock Images, cover (center), cover (left),
4–5, 6, 13, 17, 21, 21 (top); Eric Isselee/Shutterstock Images,
cover (top); Michiel de Wit/Shutterstock Images, cover (right);
CLS Design/Shutterstock Images, 9; David P. Lewis/Shutterstock
Images, 11; Ethan Daniels/Shutterstock Images, 14; Tony
Campbell/Shutterstock Images, 19; Matej Ziak/Shutterstock
Images, 21 (middle left); Bruce MacQueen/Shutterstock Images,
21 (middle right); Brian Lasenby/Shutterstock Images, 21 (right)

ISBN 9781626872981
LCCN 2014930651

Printed in the United States of America
Mankato, MN
July, 2014
PA02218

ABOUT THE AUTHOR

Lauren Coss is a writer and editor from Minnesota, land of 10,000 lakes and plenty of ponds! When she was a kid, she even kept two pond friends as pets. They were a couple of red-bellied turtles.

CONTENTS

Welcome to a Pond

It is a summer day at the pond. Can you hear the *ribbit* of the pond frogs? What about the chatter of a red wing blackbird? Dragonflies zoom between cattails. The water seems perfectly still. But then,

Many dragonflies have brightly colored bodies.

splash! A bass fish jumps out of the water. It snaps up a mayfly.

This pond is a water biome. A biome is a place in nature that supports certain types of life. Plants and animals of a biome are specially suited to live there. Let's explore the pond biome!

What Is a Pond?

Ponds are small pools of freshwater. This water is not salty like ocean water. Ponds are found all over the world. Their water is usually very still.

Many kinds of plants grow in and near ponds.

Ponds are also very shallow. Most ponds are less than 7 feet (2 m) deep. Sunlight usually reaches a pond's bottom. The sunlight helps water plants grow. Most ponds have plants growing all the way across the pond. Ponds are full of life.

A pond's water temperature is usually close to the air's temperature. This is because a pond is so shallow. The water is mostly the same temperature from top to bottom. But water temperatures in a pond can change very quickly.

Plants and animals living in ponds have to be ready for changing temperatures. In very cold places, whole ponds might freeze. This kills many of the plants and animals living there.

A Pond Forms

Ponds form in many different ways. Glaciers formed some ponds. Huge ice sheets once covered many parts of the world. Sometimes chunks of ice broke off as the glaciers moved across the land. The chunks left holes in the ground when they melted. These holes filled with water. Smaller holes became ponds.

Other ponds formed from oceans. Millions of years ago, the world's oceans were in different places than they are today. As the seas shifted, land that was once underwater dried out. But some water stayed trapped in low areas.

Rivers have also formed ponds. Rivers sometimes change course. They leave behind small ponds as they move.

Many ponds have been around a long time. Other ponds only last a few months. Some ponds form in the spring. Melted snow and rain fill these ponds. But ponds usually dry up in the summer when the weather gets warmer.

Humans make ponds, too. Farmers create ponds on their land. They dig holes in the ground. Runoff from rainwater eventually fills the holes. The ponds provide water for farm animals. Farmers also use pond water to put out wildfires. Some humans create ponds just for fun. They fish and canoe in the small ponds.

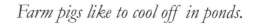

Farm pigs like to cool off in ponds.

Beaver Ponds

Humans are not the only pond builders around. Beavers live in North America, Europe, and Asia. Beaver families live in a structure called a lodge. They build it from mud and sticks. It is shaped a little like an igloo. The entrance is underwater.

Beavers like still water for their lodges. They usually live in lakes, ponds, and marshes. But sometimes only moving water is nearby. The beavers must build a pond. They make a dam in a river or stream. Beavers use mud, sticks, and logs to build a dam. The dam blocks the moving water. This creates a still pond behind the dam.

Beaver ponds quickly become homes to other pond life. Water plants begin growing. Ducks come to feed

Dead trees are good for a pond biome. Trees flooded by beaver dams die. Woodpeckers peck holes in the dead trees. They look for bugs to eat. Birds also build nests in the dead trees.

Many plants grow in the still water of a beaver's pond.

on the plants. Mosquitoes and other insects also come to the ponds. They lay their eggs in the calm waters. Dragonflies and larger insects come to eat the smaller insects. Fish, frogs, birds, and other animals come to feed on the larger insects.

At the Edge

A pond is an important **habitat** for life in the water. But many plants and animals near a pond also rely on it. Cattails often grow near a pond. Irises with beautiful purple or yellow flowers pop up at the pond's edge. During wet times, the plants' roots may be underwater. But during dry times the water is lower. Iris roots are buried in dry land.

Many land animals come to ponds to drink. Some also come to eat. Raccoons search for frogs, insects, and other animals. Moose might come to munch on water plants. Kingfishers dive into the water. These birds eat small fish and frogs. Water shrews dig holes in the banks of a pond. This is where they live. The shrews are great swimmers. They dive into the water to hunt for food. They eat small water animals and insects.

A kingfisher bird plucks a small fish from the water.

On the Surface

Ponds are usually split into three main parts. Some plants and animals live at the surface of the pond. Some live in the middle. And some settle into the muddy bottom. Many plants and animals spend time in all three parts. Ducks float on the pond's surface. But they also flip underwater to eat plants and small

Lilies and other plants grow on a pond's surface.

animals. They find food in the pond's middle and bottom.

Pond skaters are carnivores. This means they eat meat. Pond skaters eat other insects.

The surface of a pond is often covered with plants. The flat leaves of water lilies float on the water. But their roots go all the way to the pond's bottom. In summer, white or yellow flowers open. Water lilies help many pond creatures. Lily pads provide shade on hot summer days. Frogs and insects relax on top of the floating leaves. Insects and snails lay eggs under the leaves. Pond skaters skate between the leaves.

Tiny duckweed plants grow very thick on some ponds. Duckweed looks a little like a floating, green carpet. Ponds may also be covered with tiny algae. These **organisms** are small. Some are the size of a pinhead. Others are too small to see without a **microscope**. Algae can completely fill some ponds. Algae are important parts of a pond community. Bacteria, snails, **tadpoles**, and baby fish eat algae.

Life in the Middle

Just beneath the surface of a pond is open water. Some of the most common creatures in the open water are also the smallest. **Plankton** are tiny organisms that drift in the water. They are important food for bigger animals.

Baby frogs are called tadpoles. Tadpoles do not have arms or legs when they first hatch. Instead they have tails. As tadpoles get bigger, they grow arms and legs. After a few months, tadpoles hop out of the water. They are now frogs!

Many insects also live in the open water. Giant water bugs can grow to be 4 inches (10 cm) long. These fast swimmers dive into ponds to find other insects, tadpoles, and even small fish.

But even these fierce **predators** have to be careful. Fish, birds, and other larger animals hunt for giant water bugs. Fish are very common in the open water. Different kinds live in different ponds. Bluegills, sunfish, perch, carp, and bass are common in North American ponds.

Birds, such as heron and kingfishers, rely on these fish for food.

Fish aren't the only large pond animals. Frogs, newts, toads, and other **amphibians** hatch and grow underwater. As adults, they can live on dry land. But they stay close to the water. That's where they hunt for insects, small fish, and other **prey**. Ponds are also home to many reptiles, such as turtles and snakes.

Many toads live in wet habitats, such as ponds.

The Muddy Bottom

The bottom of a pond is also full of life. Many insects and their babies live in the mud. Some are herbivores. They only eat plants. Others are hunters. The water scorpion is a fierce predator. This insect hunts baby dragonflies and other small insects.

Snails snack on algae on the pond's bottom. Blood-sucking leeches wriggle in the water. Crayfish spend their days hiding under rocks. Crayfish are omnivores. They eat both plants and animals. They are also nocturnal. They are most active at night.

Bigger animals live on the bottom, too. Snapping turtles can grow to be more than 1 foot (0.3 m) long. They dig into the pond's bottom or hide in plants.

A common snapping turtle suns itself on a log.

In the winter, bottom dwellers get some new neighbors. Other turtles and frogs dig into the mud. They should stay warm enough there to survive the cold winter.

The Pond Food Chain

Many different plants and animals live in the pond biome. Each is an important part of a pond's food chain. This is the way that plants and animals work together in a habitat.

A pond's food chain begins with the sun. The sun helps plants grow. Many tiny insects and plankton come to feed on these plants. Larger insects eat the smaller ones. Fish, birds, and reptiles eat the larger insects. Raccoons, muskrats, and large birds eat the fish.

Ponds support many plants and animals. Each plant or animal is very important to this water biome. Without one plant or animal, a pond would not be the same.

Sun

Algae

Tadpole

Sunfish

Loon

In one kind of pond food chain, loons eat sunfish, sunfish eat tadpoles, tadpoles eat algae, and algae use the sun's energy to grow.

21

GLOSSARY

amphibians (am-FIB-ee-uhnz) Amphibians are cold-blooded animals with backbones that live in the water when they are young and on land as adults. Frogs and newts are amphibians.

habitat (HAB-i-tat) The environment in which an animal usually lives is its habitat. A pond is an important habitat for animals such as beavers, fish, and ducks.

microscope (MYE-kruh-skope) A microscope is a tool that scientists can use to see things that are too small to be seen by the naked eye. Some types of algae are so small they can only be seen with a microscope.

nocturnal (nahk-TUR-nuhl) Nocturnal animals are most active at night. Crayfish are nocturnal creatures.

organisms (OR-guh-niz-uhmz) Organisms are living plants and animals. Algae are tiny organisms.

photosynthesis (foh-toh-SIN-thi-sis) Photosynthesis is the process plants use to convert sunlight into food energy. Photosynthesis makes pond plants grow.

plankton (PLANGK-ton) Plankton are tiny plants and animals that drift in water. Plankton provide food for many pond animals.

predators (PRED-uh-tur) Predators are animals that hunt other animals for food. Giant water bugs are deadly pond predators.

prey (PRAY) Prey are animals that are hunted for food by other animals. A water scorpion's prey are usually dragonfly babies and other water insects.

tadpoles (TAD-poles) Tadpoles are baby frogs that live in water and use gills to breathe. Many tadpoles live in ponds and eat algae.

TO LEARN MORE

BOOKS

Franklin, Yvonne. *Ponds: Biomes and Ecosystems*. Huntington Beach, CA: Teacher Created Materials, 2009.

King, Zelda. *Examining Pond Habitats*. New York: Rosen, 2009.

Murray, Pete. *Frogs*. Mankato, MN: The Child's World, 2006.

WEB SITES

Visit our Web site for links about the pond biome:
childsworld.com/links

Note to Parents, Teachers, and Librarians: We routinely verify our Web links to make sure they are safe and active sites. So encourage your readers to check them out!

INDEX